INSIDE GUIDES

OCEAN

Written by
MIRANDA MACQUITTY

DK PUBLISHING, INC.

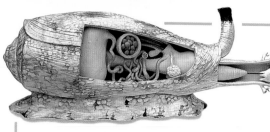

Cone snail
killing a fish

Chambered nautilus

A DK PUBLISHING BOOK

Project editor Susila Baybars
Senior art editor Dominic Zwemmer
DTP designer Nicola Studdart
Managing editor Linda Martin
Senior managing art editor Julia Harris
Picture research Monica Allende
Production Charlotte Traill
US editor Camela Decaire
Photography Geoff Brightling
Modelmaker Peter Minister Model FX

First American Edition, 1997
2 4 6 8 10 9 7 5 3 1

Published in the United States
by DK Publishing, Inc.
95 Madison Avenue, New York, New York 10016

The publishers would like to state that the colors used for
internal organs throughout the book are not realistic

A catalog record for this book is available
from the Library of Congress.
ISBN 0-7894-2035-X

Reproduced in Italy by G.R.B. Graphica, Verona
Printed in Singapore by Toppan

Angler fish

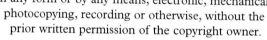
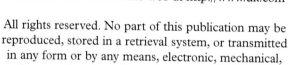

Great scallop

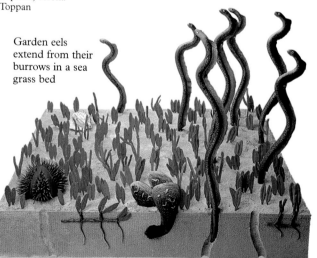

Dragonfish

Squid

American
lobster

Garden eels
extend from their
burrows in a sea
grass bed

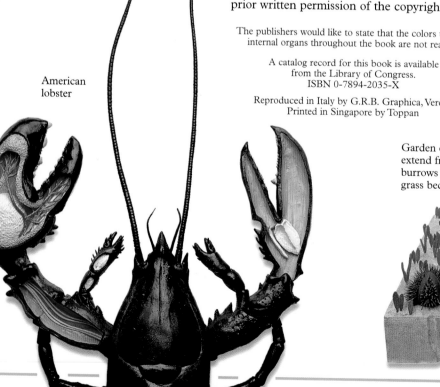

Contents

Sea horse

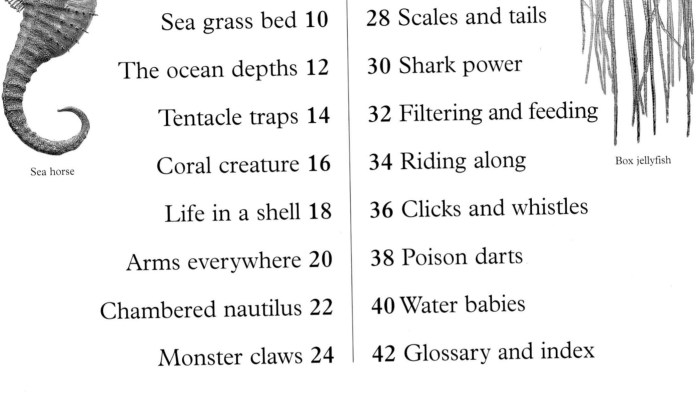

Box jellyfish

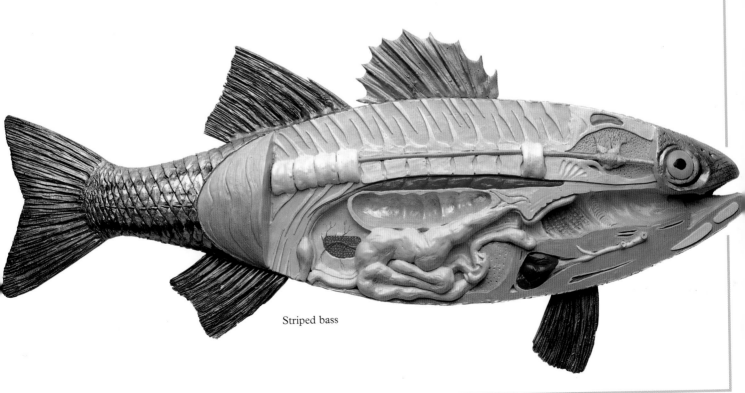

Striped bass

The watery world

On the surface, the sea seems just a vast expanse of blue, but beneath the waves there is an incredible variety of life. Plants grow in the sunlit surface waters, where they make food using energy from the sunlight. Many animals also live in the sunlit zone because of its rich supply of food. Around 656 ft (200 m) below the surface, the light begins to fade and the water becomes colder. Some animals, such as certain squid, spend the day in this twilight zone, but journey upward to feed at night. Below 3,281 ft (1,000 m), in the dark zone, there is no light and almost all the animals rely on food raining down from above. Only the vent communities in the depths generate their own source of food.

Giant kelp forest
Kelps are large brown seaweeds that grow well on rocks in shallow water to form a dense canopy. The giant kelp can grow at a rate of 1 ft (0.3 m) a day, to reach a length of over 164 ft (50 m).

Continental shelf
An area of shallow water surrounds the coast.

Volcanic islands
These form when one of the Earth's plates is pushed under another.

Trench

Shaping the seabed
This model shows the seafloor in the Atlantic Ocean off the northeastern coast of South America. As happens above sea level, a variety of processes are shaping the landscape of the seafloor. The outwash of sediment from the land cascades down the continental slope, to accumulate at the bottom. An arc of volcanic islands has formed as one of the Earth's plates is forced under another.

Continental slope
This is at the edge of the continental shelf and descends steeply into the ocean depths.

Body coloring
The silvery-black body makes gigantura harder to see in the gloom.

Deep-sea fish
Equipped with sharp-pointed teeth, gigantura preys on other creatures swimming in the depths. This slimline fish has a stretchy stomach to make room for large meals.

Binocular eyes
These tubular eyes with their big lenses work like binoculars to spot the light organs of prey.

8

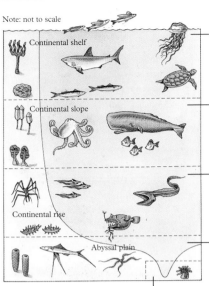

Note: not to scale
Continental shelf
Continental slope
Continental rise
Abyssal plain

Sunlit zone
Between 0–656 ft (0–200 m), the water temperature changes with the seasons.

Twilight zone
Between 656–3,280 ft (200–1,000 m), the light begins to fade and the water temperature drops.

Dark zone
Between 3,280–13,123 ft (1,000–4,000 m), it is pitch black and the water temperature is very cold.

Abyss
Between 13,123–19,685 ft (4,000–6,000 m), it is dark and cold.

Deep-sea trench
Below 19,685 ft (6,000 m), there is still life.

Ocean zones
Scientists divide the open water and the seabed into zones. The differences in the availabilty of light and the water temperature determine the kinds of creatures found there.

Phytoplankton
These microscopic plants are at the base of the ocean's food chain. They grow in the sunlit surface waters, where they are eaten by small creatures. These in turn are eaten by fish.

Ducking and diving
This harbor seal dives down to depths of 295 ft (90 m) to feed on fish. Seals are agile underwater swimmers, but they must come to the surface to breathe. They also come out of the water to give birth to and care for their pups.

Twilight swimmer
Hatchet fish are specially adapted to live in the twilight zone. Large eyes make the most of the poor light, and light organs on their undersides help them blend in with the light filtering down from above, hiding them from predators below.

Abyssal plain

Mid-Atlantic ridge

Tentacles
These push food into the mouth.

Fracture zone
New ocean floor created at the mid-Atlantic ridge causes deep cracks to appear in the Earth's surface.

Deep-sea cucumber
These sea cucumbers live in herds. They use their long, pointed tube feet to stroll around the soft seabed, where they feed on food particles buried in the sediment.

Abyssal plain
The flat floor of the deep sea is covered in a thick layer of sediment called ooze.

Sediment
Matter that is eroded from the land and carried into the ocean by rivers accumulates at the bottom of the continental slope.

Hot-water vents
Giant tube worms are among the creatures that crowd around hot-water vents in the ocean floor. All the animals in the vent community depend on bacteria, which make food using the hydrogen sulfide in the vent water. In some animals, such as tube worms, the bacteria actually live inside their bodies.

Sea grass bed

In the sunlit shallows of warm seas, meadows of flowering sea grasses flourish. Unlike seaweeds, sea grasses have proper roots through which they absorb nutrients. They grow mainly in sheltered areas, where they provide cover and food for many animals. Some creatures graze on the materials, such as seaweeds, that grow on the sea grass blades. Others benefit from the rich nutrients that are released when the blades die back and rot. One of the most beautiful kinds of fish that live among sea grasses are garden eels. The eels spend their lives in burrows in the sand, coming out to feed on tiny creatures drifting by in the currents. This model shows creatures living in a sea grass bed in the Red Sea.

Whiskers
These are used to find food on the seabed.

Dugong
Not blessed with good looks, it is hard to believe that dugongs were once mistaken for mermaids by sailors of old. These mammals feed on the roots of sea grasses, digging their snouts into the sand to find the best parts.

Three-cornered conch
This oddly shaped sea snail crawls across the sandy seabed. Conches graze on fine seaweeds that grow on the blades of sea grasses and on the surface of the sand.

Up to 10,000 eels can live in a colony

Nobs
The large, rounded nodules give the conch its name.

Green turtle
This is the only sea turtle that is an herbivore. It feeds on seaweeds and sea grasses. Like all turtles, green turtles come ashore to lay their eggs in the sand during the breeding season. They may travel great distances to return to the beaches where they themselves hatched.

Gracious urchin
This urchin can disguise itself with bits of sea grass or shells held by its tube feet. It grazes on sea grasses and seaweeds.

Keep clear
The urchin's sharp spines help deter predators.

Turtle grass
There are many kinds of sea grasses, such as surf grass, eel grass, and turtle grass. The different varieties show distinct leaf, flower, and seed shapes. This turtle grass grows in the southern Pacific Ocean near the islands of Fiji.

Empty burrow
The fragile eel burrow is lined with slime.

Underground stem
Stems spread out in a complex network just beneath the sand.

Grass roots
Roots anchor the grass in the sand.

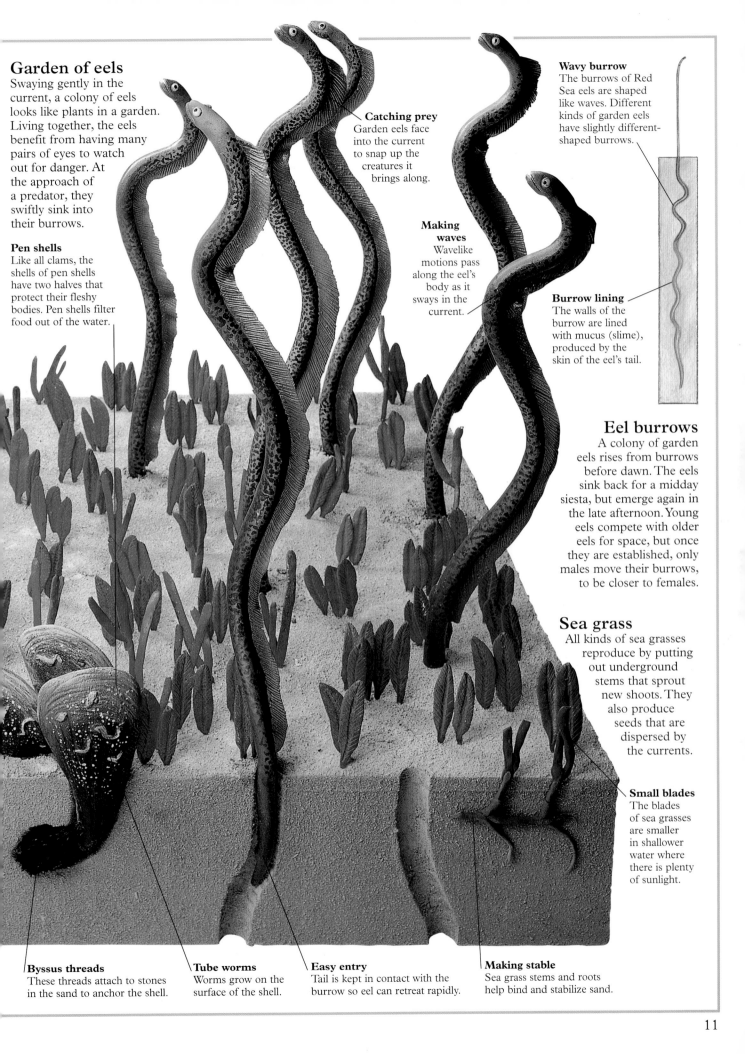

Garden of eels
Swaying gently in the current, a colony of eels looks like plants in a garden. Living together, the eels benefit from having many pairs of eyes to watch out for danger. At the approach of a predator, they swiftly sink into their burrows.

Pen shells
Like all clams, the shells of pen shells have two halves that protect their fleshy bodies. Pen shells filter food out of the water.

Catching prey
Garden eels face into the current to snap up the creatures it brings along.

Making waves
Wavelike motions pass along the eel's body as it sways in the current.

Wavy burrow
The burrows of Red Sea eels are shaped like waves. Different kinds of garden eels have slightly different-shaped burrows.

Burrow lining
The walls of the burrow are lined with mucus (slime), produced by the skin of the eel's tail.

Eel burrows
A colony of garden eels rises from burrows before dawn. The eels sink back for a midday siesta, but emerge again in the late afternoon. Young eels compete with older eels for space, but once they are established, only males move their burrows, to be closer to females.

Sea grass
All kinds of sea grasses reproduce by putting out underground stems that sprout new shoots. They also produce seeds that are dispersed by the currents.

Small blades
The blades of sea grasses are smaller in shallower water where there is plenty of sunlight.

Byssus threads
These threads attach to stones in the sand to anchor the shell.

Tube worms
Worms grow on the surface of the shell.

Easy entry
Tail is kept in contact with the burrow so eel can retreat rapidly.

Making stable
Sea grass stems and roots help bind and stabilize sand.

The ocean depths

Dark, cold, and with little food, surprisingly the ocean depths are home to a great variety of creatures – from humble sponges to monstrous-looking fish. Some animals swim just above the ocean floor, others crawl along the bottom or are anchored to the spot. Still more are hidden within the soft sediment of the seabed. Much of the sediment is made up of the skeletons of tiny plants and animals that once drifted in the surface waters. Over millions of years these remains have sunk, slowly building up to form a thick layer called ooze.

Tripod fish
These extraordinary looking fish keep their bodies clear of the soft ocean floor by resting on their long fin rays. This is also a good position from which to ambush prey drifting by in the bottom currents.

Tail fin
Fin rays from the tail fin support the end of the body.

Sea pen
Belonging to the same group as anemones and jellyfish, sea pens get their name because some look like quill pens. This kind lives at depths down to 19,685 ft (6,000 m).

Fronds
The palmlike fronds of the sea pen waft in the currents, trapping food particles.

Fin rays
Fish rests on a "tripod" of extended fin rays.

Venus's flower basket
Glass sponges are common in many areas of the ocean, from the edge of the continental shelf to depths of 19,685 ft (6,000 m) or more. The skeletons of Venus's flower baskets are made of glasslike needles of silica. The cleaned skeletons are prized by collectors.

Food collection
Water containing food particles is drawn through the pores on the sides and on the sieve plate at the top of the sponge.

Sediment
This is made up of the remains of plants and creatures.

Growing high
One kind of Venus's flower basket can grow up to 23 in (60 cm) tall.

Twisted strands of silica

Bulblike base
This expands and contracts to dig down into the soft ocean floor.

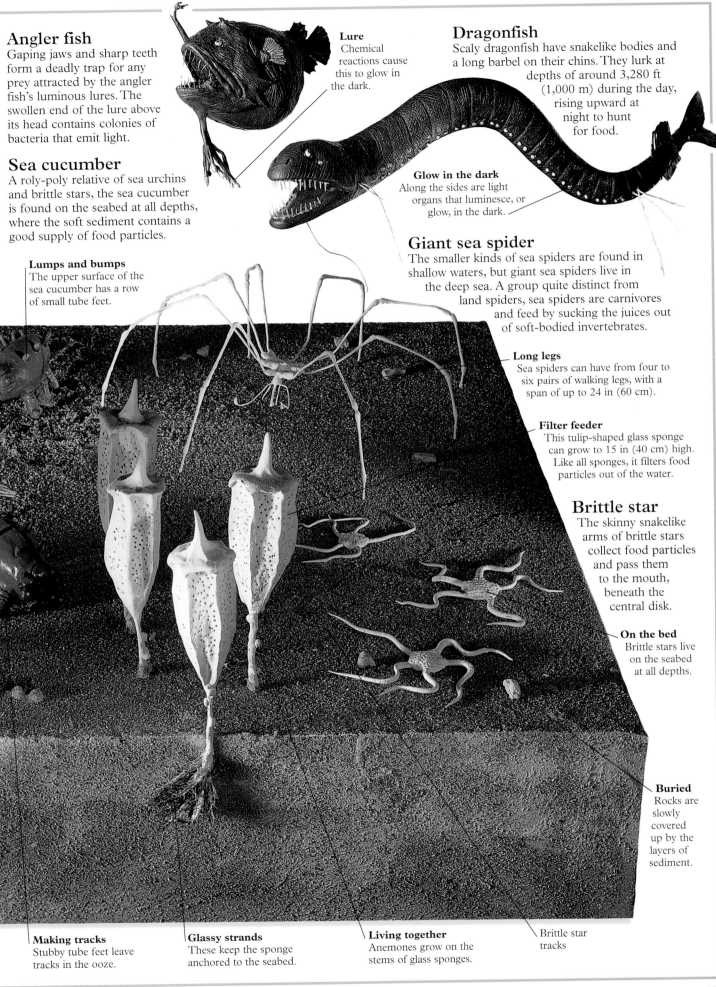

Angler fish
Gaping jaws and sharp teeth form a deadly trap for any prey attracted by the angler fish's luminous lures. The swollen end of the lure above its head contains colonies of bacteria that emit light.

Sea cucumber
A roly-poly relative of sea urchins and brittle stars, the sea cucumber is found on the seabed at all depths, where the soft sediment contains a good supply of food particles.

Lumps and bumps
The upper surface of the sea cucumber has a row of small tube feet.

Lure
Chemical reactions cause this to glow in the dark.

Dragonfish
Scaly dragonfish have snakelike bodies and a long barbel on their chins. They lurk at depths of around 3,280 ft (1,000 m) during the day, rising upward at night to hunt for food.

Glow in the dark
Along the sides are light organs that luminesce, or glow, in the dark.

Giant sea spider
The smaller kinds of sea spiders are found in shallow waters, but giant sea spiders live in the deep sea. A group quite distinct from land spiders, sea spiders are carnivores and feed by sucking the juices out of soft-bodied invertebrates.

Long legs
Sea spiders can have from four to six pairs of walking legs, with a span of up to 24 in (60 cm).

Filter feeder
This tulip-shaped glass sponge can grow to 15 in (40 cm) high. Like all sponges, it filters food particles out of the water.

Brittle star
The skinny snakelike arms of brittle stars collect food particles and pass them to the mouth, beneath the central disk.

On the bed
Brittle stars live on the seabed at all depths.

Buried
Rocks are slowly covered up by the layers of sediment.

Making tracks
Stubby tube feet leave tracks in the ooze.

Glassy strands
These keep the sponge anchored to the seabed.

Living together
Anemones grow on the stems of glass sponges.

Brittle star tracks

Tentacle traps

Jellyfish have a simple bag-shaped body made of a jellylike substance and long tentacles armed with tiny stinging cells called nematocysts. They are cnidarians and, like their relatives the corals and anemones, jellyfish have only one body opening to both take in food and pass out waste. Unlike anemones and corals, which grow on rocks, jellyfish swim and drift with the currents. All jellyfish can sting, but only a few kinds possess venom strong enough to cause serious injury to people. The most vicious and deadly of these is the box jellyfish, which lives in the warm waters off northern Australia and southeastern Asia.

Moon jellyfish

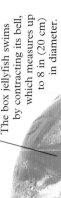

The moon jellyfish has weak, ineffective stings, so it uses the sticky slime on the undersurface of its bell to trap small prey. The prey is wiped off the bell by fleshy arms located around the mouth.

Box-shaped bell
The box jellyfish swims by contracting its bell, which measures up to 8 in (20 cm) in diameter.

Bunch of tentacles
Four bases sprout up to 15 tentacles each.

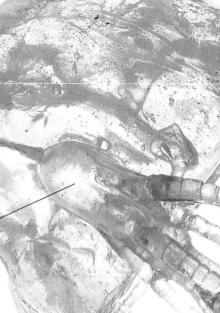
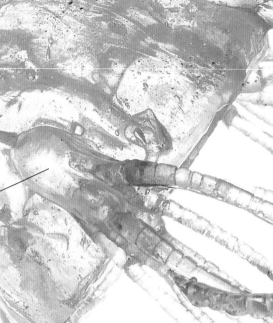
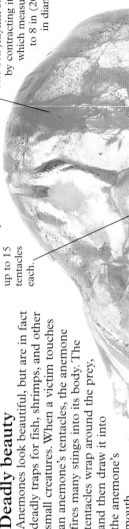

Deadly beauty

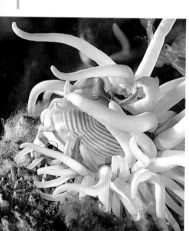

Anemones look beautiful, but are in fact deadly traps for fish, shrimps, and other small creatures. When a victim touches an anemone's tentacles, the anemone fires many stings into its body. The tentacles wrap around the prey, and then draw it into the anemone's mouth.

Fire coral

Fire corals often grow on coral reefs, but are not in fact true corals. Instead, they belong to a group called the sea firs. If a diver brushes against a piece of fire coral by mistake, he or she may get a painful rash from its stings.

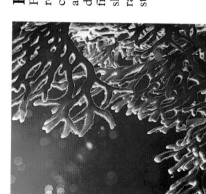

Tentacles
These may trail behind the jellyfish for over 10 ft (3 m). They coil up to trap small prey, which are then passed to the mouth.

Fish victim
The barbed tubes released from the tiny nematocysts pierce through the fish's scales and penetrate the flesh to a depth of 0.02 in (0.5 mm).

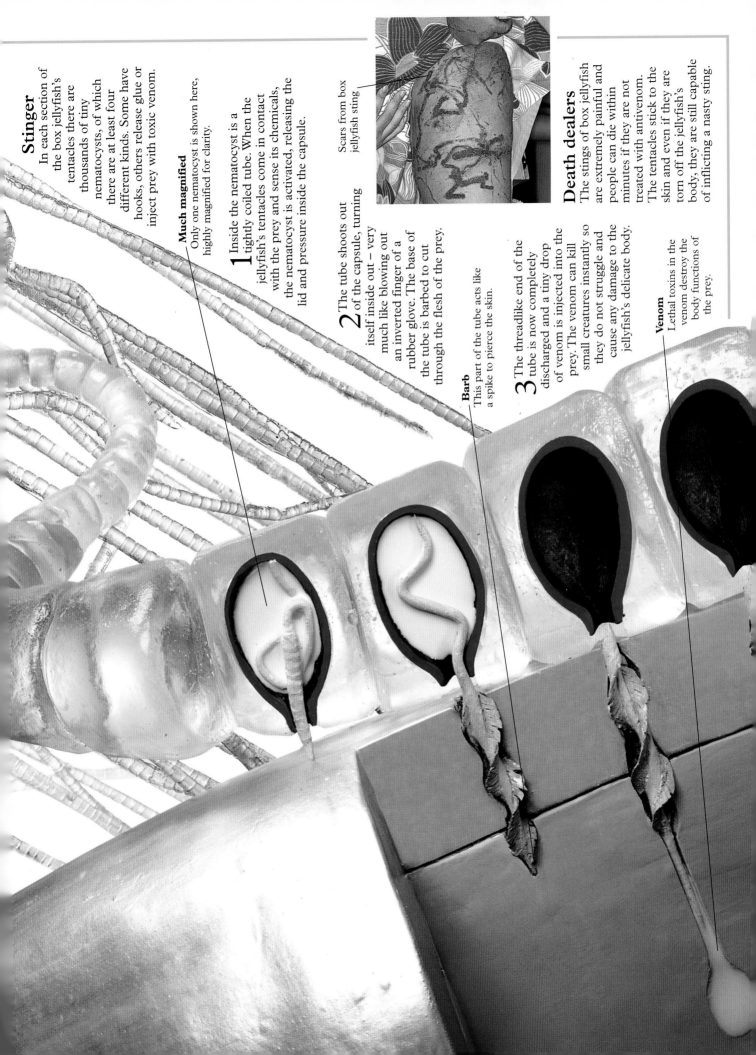

Stinger

In each section of the box jellyfish's tentacles there are thousands of tiny nematocysts, of which there are at least four different kinds. Some have hooks, others release glue or inject prey with toxic venom.

Much magnified

Only one nematocyst is shown here, highly magnified for clarity.

1 Inside the nematocyst is a tightly coiled tube. When the jellyfish's tentacles come in contact with the prey and sense its chemicals, the nematocyst is activated, releasing the lid and pressure inside the capsule.

Scars from box jellyfish sting

2 The tube shoots out of the capsule, turning itself inside out – very much like blowing out an inverted finger of a rubber glove. The base of the tube is barbed to cut through the flesh of the prey.

Barb

This part of the tube acts like a spike to pierce the skin.

3 The threadlike end of the tube is now completely discharged and a tiny drop of venom is injected into the prey. The venom can kill small creatures instantly so they do not struggle and cause any damage to the jellyfish's delicate body.

Death dealers

The stings of box jellyfish are extremely painful and people can die within minutes if they are not treated with antivenom. The tentacles stick to the skin and even if they are torn off the jellyfish's body, they are still capable of inflicting a nasty sting.

Venom

Lethal toxins in the venom destroy the body functions of the prey.

Coral creature

Stony corals are anemonelike creatures that build hard skeletons to protect their soft bodies. Each tiny individual is called a polyp. The polyps live in colonies, with each one joined to its neighbor by a sheet of tissue. The polyps' stony skeletons build up to form coral reefs – the largest structures made by living organisms. Within the polyp's soft tissues are microscopic plants called algae, which help make their skeletons and provide some food. The algae need light to grow, so coral reefs are found in the sunlit waters of warm, tropical seas.

Life around the reef
Coral reefs swarm with life. With all its nooks and crannies, a reef provides a home for a great variety of creatures. Some feed on the coral tissues, others graze on seaweeds or devour other reef inhabitants. These anthias fish feed on tiny creatures drifting in the water.

Soft coral
Many kinds of corals do not have hard skeletons, such as soft corals. These corals have a skeleton of needlelike spikes supporting their fleshy bodies. Polyps extend from the fleshy mass to feed. Soft corals grow well where there are currents to bring them food.

Cup coral
This cup coral from Sri Lanka does not have microscopic algae inside its tissues, so it does not produce enough of a skeleton to help build a coral reef. Non reef-building corals like these are often solitary or live in small groups.

Stingers
Tentacle of polyp is armed with stinging cells.

Stony coral
The hard skeleton of a stony coral is completely covered by living tissue. The coral colony grows as new polyps bud off existing ones. Each individual polyp makes a skeleton of the mineral calcium carbonate. When the colony dies, the skeleton provides a surface for new corals to grow on.

Building upwards
Each polyp adds new layers of skeleton beneath it as it grows.

Living tissue

Hard skeleton
The cup in which the polyp sits is revealed when the living polyp tissue is taken away.

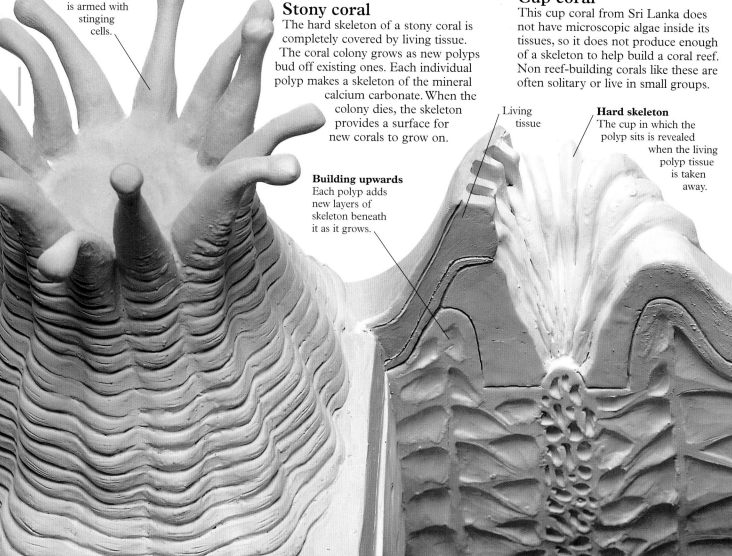

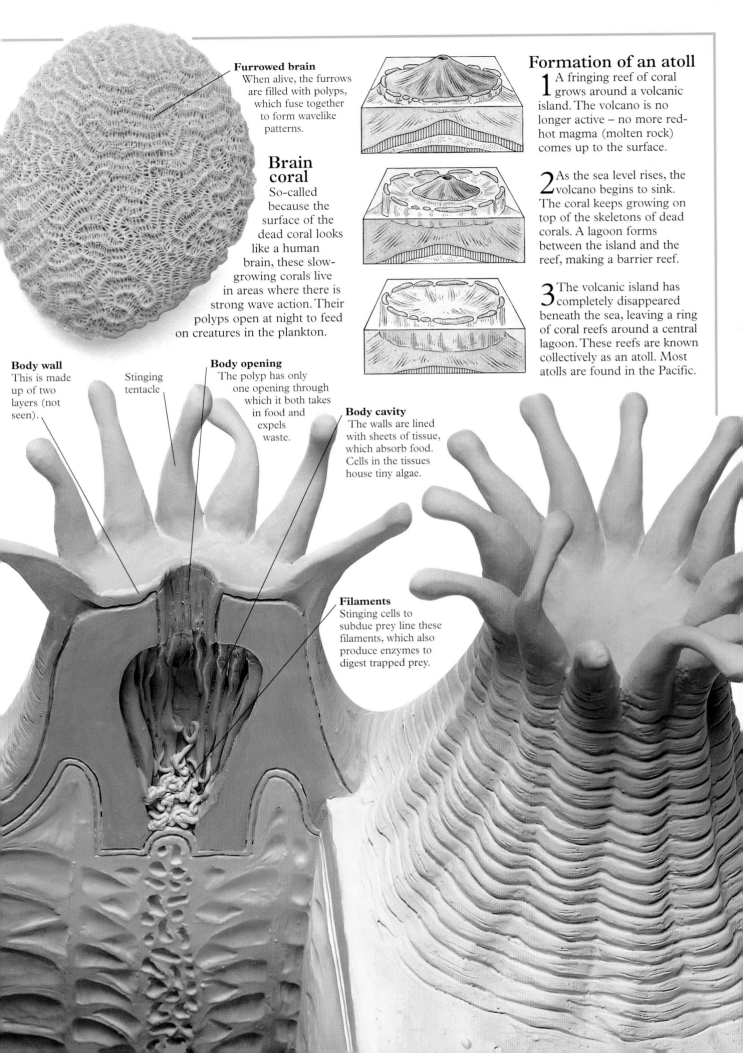

Furrowed brain
When alive, the furrows are filled with polyps, which fuse together to form wavelike patterns.

Brain coral
So-called because the surface of the dead coral looks like a human brain, these slow-growing corals live in areas where there is strong wave action. Their polyps open at night to feed on creatures in the plankton.

Formation of an atoll
1 A fringing reef of coral grows around a volcanic island. The volcano is no longer active – no more red-hot magma (molten rock) comes up to the surface.

2 As the sea level rises, the volcano begins to sink. The coral keeps growing on top of the skeletons of dead corals. A lagoon forms between the island and the reef, making a barrier reef.

3 The volcanic island has completely disappeared beneath the sea, leaving a ring of coral reefs around a central lagoon. These reefs are known collectively as an atoll. Most atolls are found in the Pacific.

Body wall
This is made up of two layers (not seen).

Stinging tentacle

Body opening
The polyp has only one opening through which it both takes in food and expels waste.

Body cavity
The walls are lined with sheets of tissue, which absorb food. Cells in the tissues house tiny algae.

Filaments
Stinging cells to subdue prey line these filaments, which also produce enzymes to digest trapped prey.

Life in a shell

The soft, squishy parts inside a scallop are protected by its hinged shell. If provoked, a single large muscle pulls each half of the shell shut in an instant. Clams with less rounded shells have two sets of muscles to pull the halves together. Scallops swim by squirting water out of their shells, whereas other clams use a foot to burrow into the seabed or are anchored to the spot. All clams are mollusks – a group with soft bodies surrounded by a layer of skin called the mantle. Most mollusks, such as snails, chitons, and nautiluses, have an outer shell. Whatever shape the shell is, it is produced by the mantle.

Giant among scallops
The great scallop is a robust clam that grows up to 5 in (13 cm) across. Like all clams, the scallop's shell is made of two halves called valves. When resting on the seabed, the body organs lie in the the lower, concave valve.

Snap shut
Contrary to popular myth, the giant clam cannot trap a person in its shell, because it closes very slowly.

Giant blue clam
This clam grows to 12 in (30 cm) across, but the giant clam itself can be much bigger. These clams feed on microscopic plants that grow in the fleshy mantle folds at the edge of the shell and by filtering food particles out of the water.

A pearl in the making

1 A particle of grit gets trapped under the shell of a pearl oyster, causing irritation.

2 The mantle (outer tissues) secretes layers of mother-of-pearl around the particle.

3 Mother-of-pearl completely surrounds the particle, forming a single pearl.

Foot
The great scallop swims rather than crawls, so its foot is not well developed.

Palps
These sort food particles and pass them to the mouth.

Testis
This produces sperm, which are shed into the water.

Intestine
Waste material passes along this tube.

Guard tentacles

Sensory tentacles

Gills
These absorb oxygen from the water. They also filter food particles, trapping them in sticky mucus. The beating of tiny hairs called cilia transport the food particles to the mouth.

Ovary
This produces eggs, which are shed into the water, where they are fertilized.

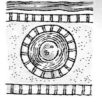

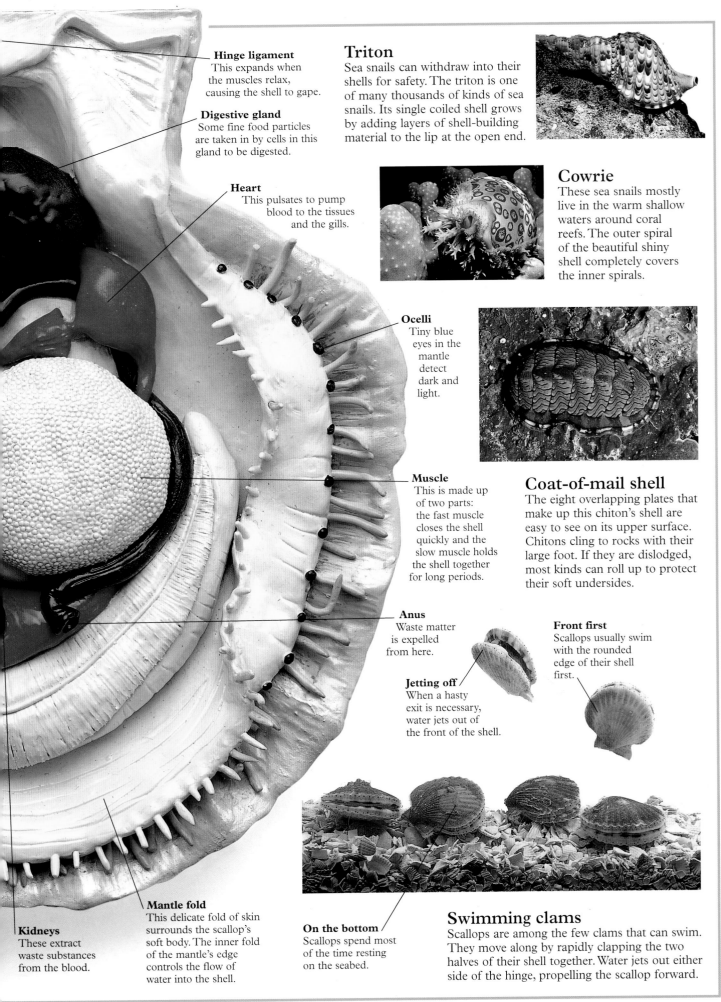

Hinge ligament
This expands when the muscles relax, causing the shell to gape.

Digestive gland
Some fine food particles are taken in by cells in this gland to be digested.

Triton
Sea snails can withdraw into their shells for safety. The triton is one of many thousands of kinds of sea snails. Its single coiled shell grows by adding layers of shell-building material to the lip at the open end.

Heart
This pulsates to pump blood to the tissues and the gills.

Cowrie
These sea snails mostly live in the warm shallow waters around coral reefs. The outer spiral of the beautiful shiny shell completely covers the inner spirals.

Ocelli
Tiny blue eyes in the mantle detect dark and light.

Muscle
This is made up of two parts: the fast muscle closes the shell quickly and the slow muscle holds the shell together for long periods.

Coat-of-mail shell
The eight overlapping plates that make up this chiton's shell are easy to see on its upper surface. Chitons cling to rocks with their large foot. If they are dislodged, most kinds can roll up to protect their soft undersides.

Anus
Waste matter is expelled from here.

Front first
Scallops usually swim with the rounded edge of their shell first.

Jetting off
When a hasty exit is necessary, water jets out of the front of the shell.

Kidneys
These extract waste substances from the blood.

Mantle fold
This delicate fold of skin surrounds the scallop's soft body. The inner fold of the mantle's edge controls the flow of water into the shell.

On the bottom
Scallops spend most of the time resting on the seabed.

Swimming clams
Scallops are among the few clams that can swim. They move along by rapidly clapping the two halves of their shell together. Water jets out either side of the hinge, propelling the scallop forward.

Arms everywhere

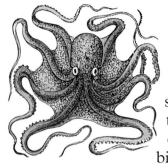

Speedy creatures of the open seas, squid dart around, powered by jets of water from their funnels. Usually squid swim backward with their arms and tentacles behind them. But when hunting, squid swim headfirst, shooting out their tentacles to grab fish or crustaceans. Squid first bite their prey and then inject it with venom to subdue it, before tearing it to pieces with their beaklike jaws. Squid, cuttlefish, octopuses, and nautiluses belong to the group of cephalopod mollusks. The name means head-footed, because every member of the group has a head surrounded by tentacles or arms. Squid and cuttlefish have eight arms and two long tentacles, octopuses have only eight arms.

Jet propulsion

Squids swim by jet propulsion. Water enters the mantle cavity on either side of the funnel. When muscles in the mantle contract, a tight seal is formed against the squid's neck and forces the water out through the funnel. Squids usually swim tail first.

Swollen cavity
The body bulges outward when the mantle cavity fills with water.

Eye
Squid have good vision.

Tentacles
The tentacles only have suckers on the spadelike ends.

Arms
The arms push food toward the mouth.

Keeping watch
Eye is used to spot prey.

Bag-shaped
Streamlined body does not have any fins.

Rows of suckers

Octopus suckers

Arranged in rows along the underside of each arm, the suckers are used to grip on to surfaces or the octopus's prey. Unlike squid suckers, octopus suckers are not on stalks and do not have horny rims or hooks.

Close to the seabed

Unlike squid, most octopuses prefer to move around slowly, staying close to the rocky seabed. If possible, they keep one arm in contact with the floor, but when under attack, they jet off rapidly with their eight arms trailing along behind.

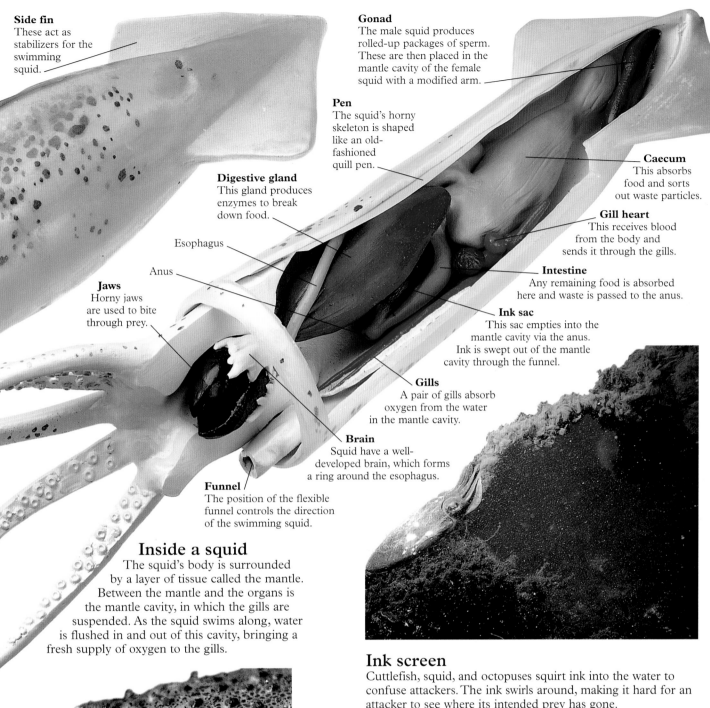

Side fin
These act as stabilizers for the swimming squid.

Gonad
The male squid produces rolled-up packages of sperm. These are then placed in the mantle cavity of the female squid with a modified arm.

Pen
The squid's horny skeleton is shaped like an old-fashioned quill pen.

Caecum
This absorbs food and sorts out waste particles.

Digestive gland
This gland produces enzymes to break down food.

Gill heart
This receives blood from the body and sends it through the gills.

Esophagus

Anus

Intestine
Any remaining food is absorbed here and waste is passed to the anus.

Jaws
Horny jaws are used to bite through prey.

Ink sac
This sac empties into the mantle cavity via the anus. Ink is swept out of the mantle cavity through the funnel.

Gills
A pair of gills absorb oxygen from the water in the mantle cavity.

Brain
Squid have a well-developed brain, which forms a ring around the esophagus.

Funnel
The position of the flexible funnel controls the direction of the swimming squid.

Inside a squid
The squid's body is surrounded by a layer of tissue called the mantle. Between the mantle and the organs is the mantle cavity, in which the gills are suspended. As the squid swims along, water is flushed in and out of this cavity, bringing a fresh supply of oxygen to the gills.

Ink screen
Cuttlefish, squid, and octopuses squirt ink into the water to confuse attackers. The ink swirls around, making it hard for an attacker to see where its intended prey has gone.

Squid attack
Sperm whales dive deep to find their awesome prey, the giant squid. These squid grow to 59 ft (18 m) long. As yet, no one has seen a giant squid swimming, but the remains of the giant squid have been found in the stomachs of whales.

Making a mark
Scars are caused by the horny-ringed suckers of the giant squid.

Light in the dark
Many squid live in the twilight zone, where there is little light. They have light organs, called photophores, along their bodies to communicate with other squid, to confuse predators, and to attract prey.

Chambered nautilus

A rare sight in the ocean, the chambered nautilus lives in water generally too deep for scuba divers to explore. Recognizable by their distinctively patterned spiral shells, there are five, possibly six, different kinds of chambered nautiluses, found in the Pacific and Indian Oceans. The gas-filled outer chambers of the shell counter the weight of the body tissues, so the nautilus stays afloat. During the day the nautilus lurks at depths of 1,312 ft (400 m), resting on the seabed. At night it rises closer to the surface and swims around the lower slopes of coral reefs in search of dead flesh and shellfish to eat.

Ammonites
These nautilus relatives were abundant in ancient seas. They died out 65 million years ago, but many preserved fossil shells have been found.

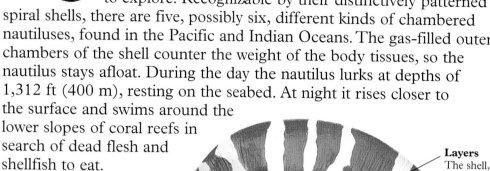

Eye
Pinhole-style eye does not have a lens.

Layers
The shell, which is produced by the mantle, is mainly made up of aragonite.

Hood
When the nautilus retreats into its shell, this tough, fleshy shield covers the entrance.

Jaws
The beaklike jaws are strong enough to crunch through shellfish.

Inner tentacles

Nautilus
The nautilus belongs to the group of cephalopod mollusks that includes squid, octopuses, and cuttlefish. Like these relatives, it swims by jet propulsion. Water is forced out of the mantle cavity as the creature retreats into its shell, contracting the flaps that form the funnel. Nautiluses usually swim backward, but they change direction to approach food tentacles first.

Outer shell
The nautilus is the only cephalopod alive today to have an outer shell.

Thin egg case
This delicate shell gives the "paper" nautilus its name.

Tentacles
Up to 90 tentacles are arranged in inner and outer rows. The tentacles do not have suckers, but are covered with a sticky mucus that helps keep hold of prey.

Paper nautilus
Also called argonauts, paper nautiluses drift in the warm surface waters of the ocean. The female makes an egg case to protect herself and her brood. Each half of the case is produced by one of a pair of broadly shaped arms. The much smaller male paper nautilus sometimes shares her egg-case home.

Funnel
Water is expelled through the funnel to provide the thrust for jet propulsion.

Mantle cavity

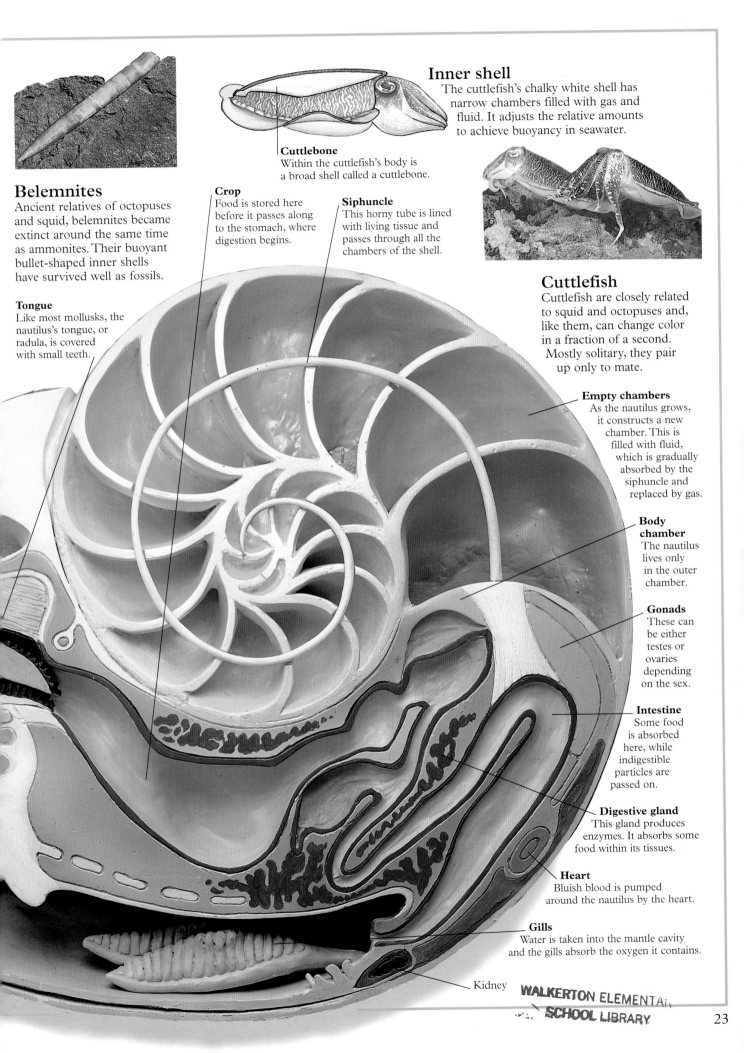

Inner shell
The cuttlefish's chalky white shell has narrow chambers filled with gas and fluid. It adjusts the relative amounts to achieve buoyancy in seawater.

Cuttlebone
Within the cuttlefish's body is a broad shell called a cuttlebone.

Belemnites
Ancient relatives of octopuses and squid, belemnites became extinct around the same time as ammonites. Their buoyant bullet-shaped inner shells have survived well as fossils.

Crop
Food is stored here before it passes along to the stomach, where digestion begins.

Siphuncle
This horny tube is lined with living tissue and passes through all the chambers of the shell.

Cuttlefish
Cuttlefish are closely related to squid and octopuses and, like them, can change color in a fraction of a second. Mostly solitary, they pair up only to mate.

Tongue
Like most mollusks, the nautilus's tongue, or radula, is covered with small teeth.

Empty chambers
As the nautilus grows, it constructs a new chamber. This is filled with fluid, which is gradually absorbed by the siphuncle and replaced by gas.

Body chamber
The nautilus lives only in the outer chamber.

Gonads
These can be either testes or ovaries depending on the sex.

Intestine
Some food is absorbed here, while indigestible particles are passed on.

Digestive gland
This gland produces enzymes. It absorbs some food within its tissues.

Heart
Bluish blood is pumped around the nautilus by the heart.

Gills
Water is taken into the mantle cavity and the gills absorb the oxygen it contains.

Kidney

Monster claws

The massive claws of a lobster are a formidable set of weapons that can give a nasty pinch. Unless cornered, however, lobsters escape by swimming backward rapidly, flapping their tails. Apart from warding off attackers, the main job of the first pair of claws is to tackle food, scavenged from the seabed. Lobsters are crustaceans, along with shrimps and crabs. All crustaceans have an outer skeleton, jointed limbs, and two pairs of feelers, called antennae, in front of their mouths. The skeleton protects their soft inner parts and provides an attachment for the muscles. The drawback of the outer skeleton is that it has to be shed to allow for growth.

Crushers and cutters

The crushing claw has a large muscle and is strong enough to crack the heavy shells of clams and snails. The cutting claw snips away at flesh. Once the flesh comes free, morsels of food are passed to the mouth.

Sharp shooter

Pistol shrimps are almost always found in pairs. They are so-called because they make snapping noises to scare away enemies. The noise is made by the sudden release of the movable finger on one claw that is especially large.

Mantis shrimp

Armed with sharply serrated claws, the mantis shrimp can both defend itself and grab at prey such as small fish and shrimps. The claws shoot out in a fraction of a second with enough force to break through glass.

Crushing teeth
More pressure can be applied by a narrow point like this than a broad surface.

Artery network
A good supply of blood brings oxygen and food to the muscles.

Nerves
The brain passes messages to and from the claws via a network of nerves.

Flexor muscle
This is the largest muscle in the claw and is responsible for its crushing power.

Small claws
The second and third pairs of legs end in pincers that are controlled by muscles.

Roving eye
The eyes are located on moving stalks.

Nerves
Signals pass along the nerves to control the claw's movements.

Walking legs
Lobsters have four pairs of walking legs.

Built for strength
The shell is strengthened by the mineral calcium carbonate.

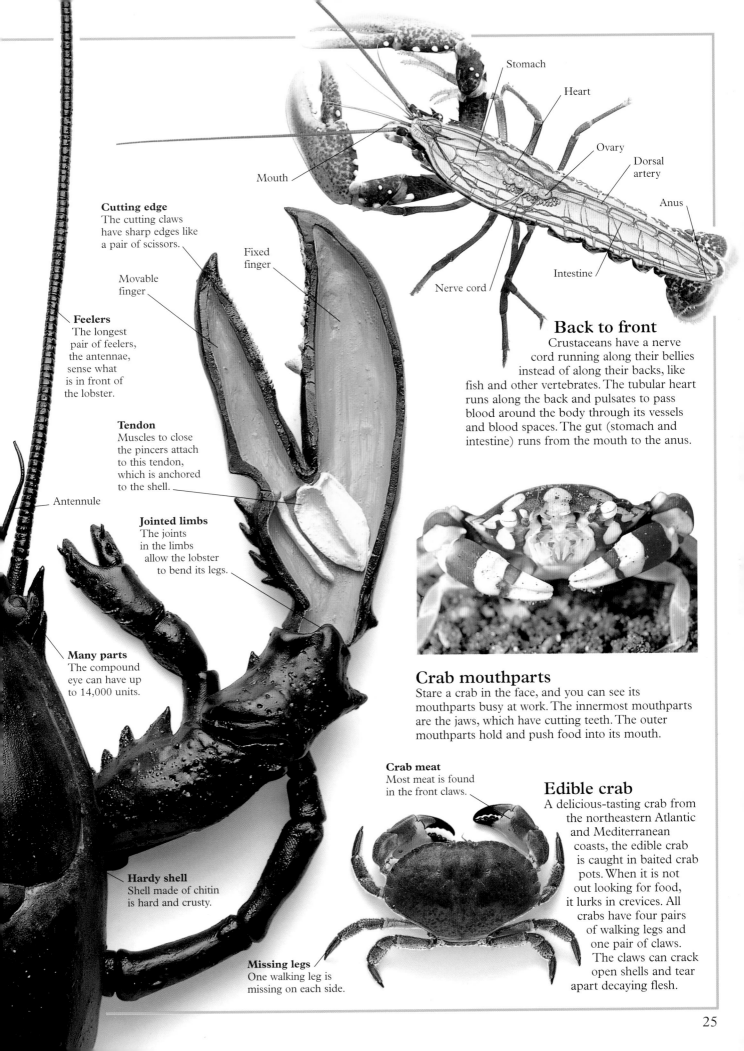

Stomach

Heart

Ovary

Dorsal artery

Anus

Mouth

Intestine

Nerve cord

Cutting edge
The cutting claws have sharp edges like a pair of scissors.

Fixed finger

Movable finger

Feelers
The longest pair of feelers, the antennae, sense what is in front of the lobster.

Antennule

Tendon
Muscles to close the pincers attach to this tendon, which is anchored to the shell.

Jointed limbs
The joints in the limbs allow the lobster to bend its legs.

Many parts
The compound eye can have up to 14,000 units.

Hardy shell
Shell made of chitin is hard and crusty.

Missing legs
One walking leg is missing on each side.

Back to front
Crustaceans have a nerve cord running along their bellies instead of along their backs, like fish and other vertebrates. The tubular heart runs along the back and pulsates to pass blood around the body through its vessels and blood spaces. The gut (stomach and intestine) runs from the mouth to the anus.

Crab mouthparts
Stare a crab in the face, and you can see its mouthparts busy at work. The innermost mouthparts are the jaws, which have cutting teeth. The outer mouthparts hold and push food into its mouth.

Crab meat
Most meat is found in the front claws.

Edible crab
A delicious-tasting crab from the northeastern Atlantic and Mediterranean coasts, the edible crab is caught in baited crab pots. When it is not out looking for food, it lurks in crevices. All crabs have four pairs of walking legs and one pair of claws. The claws can crack open shells and tear apart decaying flesh.

25

Spiny ball

Hundreds of spines make a sea urchin a prickly mouthful, so many predators prefer to leave them well alone. Relatives of sea urchins include brittle stars, sea cucumbers, and starfish. These are all echinoderms, a name which means spiny-skinned, although sea cucumbers do not have spines. All echinoderms have a five-rayed body plan. Another common feature is their circulatory system, which is filled with a fluid much like seawater. This canal system transports substances around the body and fluid to the tube feet. The sea urchin uses its tube feet and spines to crawl along. Sea urchins do not have a brain, but coordinate their actions via a raylike network of nerves.

Urchin shell
The test (shell) is made up of interlocking plates, which protect the sea urchin's soft inner parts.

Radial nerve

Spines
A ball-and-socket joint allows the spines to move in all directions.

Tube feet
Tipped with suckers, the tube feet can grip on to surfaces.

Tube feet bases
The bases of the tube feet are connected by a canal. When the bases contract, fluid enters the tube feet, making them longer.

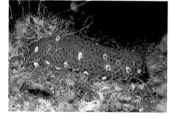

Exploding stomach
Some sea cucumbers spew out sticky tubes, or even their guts and breathing structures, when provoked. The sea cucumber can then crawl away from its attacker. After a while its internal organs grow back.

Starfish
The starfish's five arms grow from a central disk. Underneath the arms are two rows of tube feet. The starfish uses its tube feet to walk along and to grip on to prey. Beneath its spiny skin is a series of bony plates.

Aristotle's lantern
The urchin's complex feeding mechanism is named after the famous philosopher from ancient Greece, who likened the whole animal to a lamp. Sets of muscles operate five teeth that surround the mouth. The teeth can move in various directions to graze on seaweeds, sea mats, and other small animals that grow on hard surfaces.

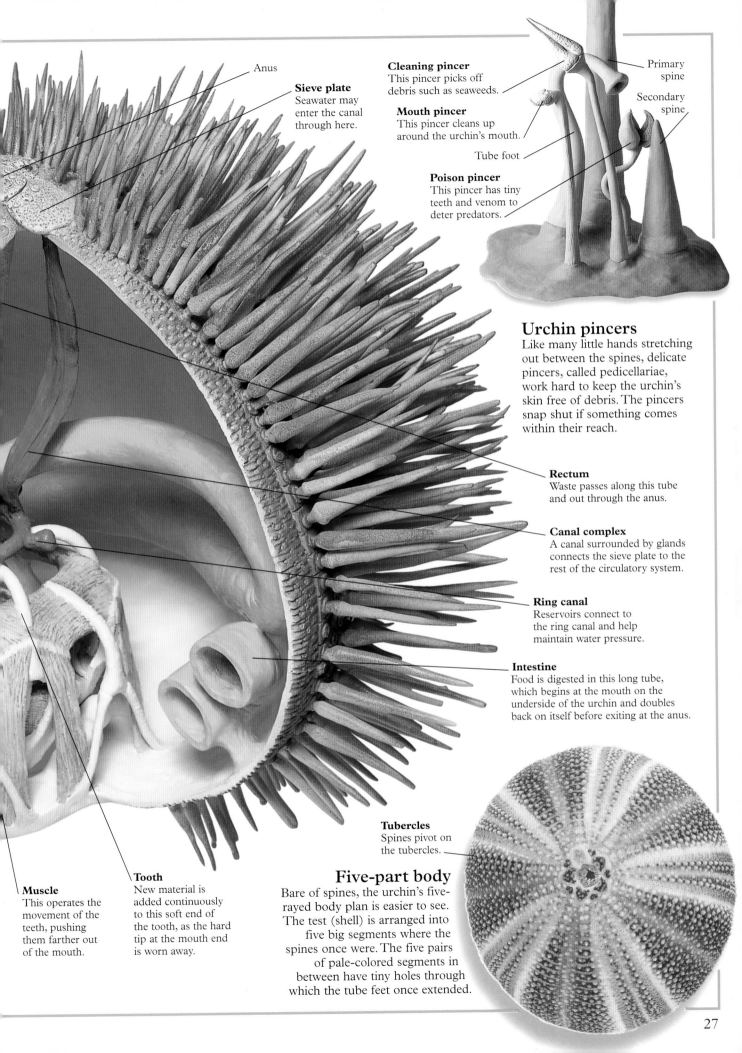

Anus

Sieve plate
Seawater may
enter the canal
through here.

Cleaning pincer
This pincer picks off
debris such as seaweeds.

Mouth pincer
This pincer cleans up
around the urchin's mouth.

Poison pincer
This pincer has tiny
teeth and venom to
deter predators.

Primary
spine

Secondary
spine

Tube foot

Urchin pincers
Like many little hands stretching
out between the spines, delicate
pincers, called pedicellariae,
work hard to keep the urchin's
skin free of debris. The pincers
snap shut if something comes
within their reach.

Rectum
Waste passes along this tube
and out through the anus.

Canal complex
A canal surrounded by glands
connects the sieve plate to the
rest of the circulatory system.

Ring canal
Reservoirs connect to
the ring canal and help
maintain water pressure.

Intestine
Food is digested in this long tube,
which begins at the mouth on the
underside of the urchin and doubles
back on itself before exiting at the anus.

Tubercles
Spines pivot on
the tubercles.

Muscle
This operates the
movement of the
teeth, pushing
them farther out
of the mouth.

Tooth
New material is
added continuously
to this soft end of
the tooth, as the hard
tip at the mouth end
is worn away.

Five-part body
Bare of spines, the urchin's five-
rayed body plan is easier to see.
The test (shell) is arranged into
five big segments where the
spines once were. The five pairs
of pale-colored segments in
between have tiny holes through
which the tube feet once extended.

Scales and tails

Thousands of different kinds of fish live in the sea, from its sunlit surface to its dark depths. There are three main groups: bony fish, cartilaginous fish, and jawless fish, but all fish are vertebrates, which means they have a backbone. The majority of fish in the sea are bony fish. Bony fish have a bony skeleton, a gill flap covering their gills, and scales. Most bony fish have a gas-filled swim bladder to control their level in the water. Cartilaginous fish, such as sharks and rays, have a skeleton made of cartilage, slit openings for each set of gills, and most have toothlike denticles covering the skin. Jawless fish have round mouths and long bodies that lack paired fins.

Fish anatomy
The organs of bony fish like this striped bass mostly lie below its lateral line. The rest of the body is made of large blocks of muscle. The actions of these muscles make the tail move and power the fish through the water.

Lateral line
Receptors connected to the fluid-filled canal sense vibrations in the water.

Muscle
Blocks of muscle on either side of the fish contract alternately.

Ovary
The female bass produces many eggs here. The eggs are shed into the water, where they are fertilized by sperm shed by the male.

Bony fish skeleton
A skeleton supports the fish's body and gives its muscles something to pull against. In addition, the skull protects the brain and the backbone protects the spinal cord. Bony fish have a many-jointed skeleton, which means that they can maneuver more easily than cartilaginous fish.

Cartilaginous ray
Manta rays are the largest kind of rays. They have huge, winglike fins that beat up and down. These rays filter food out of the water. Projections on the head help channel water into their open mouth as they swim along.

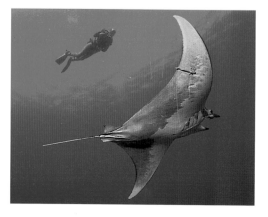

Jawless lamprey
The eellike sea lamprey is a parasite. Around its mouth are horrible horny teeth, which it uses to attach itself to the flesh of other fish so it can suck out their blood. The sea lamprey lives in the North Atlantic and migrates into freshwater habitats to spawn.

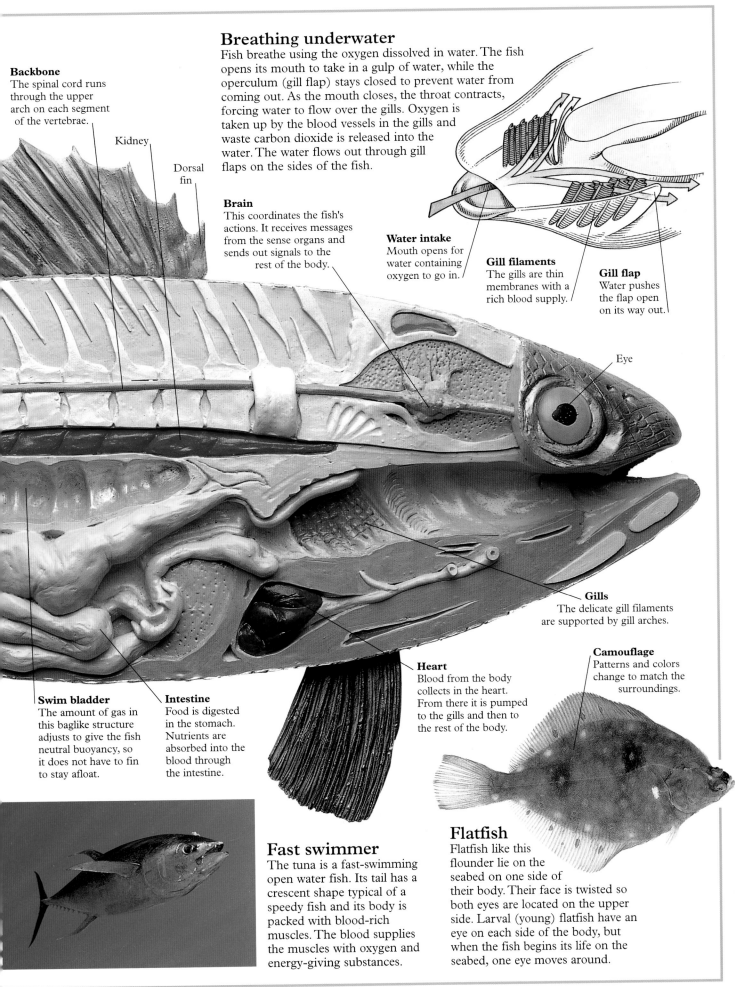

Backbone
The spinal cord runs through the upper arch on each segment of the vertebrae.

Kidney

Dorsal fin

Breathing underwater
Fish breathe using the oxygen dissolved in water. The fish opens its mouth to take in a gulp of water, while the operculum (gill flap) stays closed to prevent water from coming out. As the mouth closes, the throat contracts, forcing water to flow over the gills. Oxygen is taken up by the blood vessels in the gills and waste carbon dioxide is released into the water. The water flows out through gill flaps on the sides of the fish.

Brain
This coordinates the fish's actions. It receives messages from the sense organs and sends out signals to the rest of the body.

Water intake
Mouth opens for water containing oxygen to go in.

Gill filaments
The gills are thin membranes with a rich blood supply.

Gill flap
Water pushes the flap open on its way out.

Eye

Gills
The delicate gill filaments are supported by gill arches.

Swim bladder
The amount of gas in this baglike structure adjusts to give the fish neutral buoyancy, so it does not have to fin to stay afloat.

Intestine
Food is digested in the stomach. Nutrients are absorbed into the blood through the intestine.

Heart
Blood from the body collects in the heart. From there it is pumped to the gills and then to the rest of the body.

Camouflage
Patterns and colors change to match the surroundings.

Fast swimmer
The tuna is a fast-swimming open water fish. Its tail has a crescent shape typical of a speedy fish and its body is packed with blood-rich muscles. The blood supplies the muscles with oxygen and energy-giving substances.

Flatfish
Flatfish like this flounder lie on the seabed on one side of their body. Their face is twisted so both eyes are located on the upper side. Larval (young) flatfish have an eye on each side of the body, but when the fish begins its life on the seabed, one eye moves around.

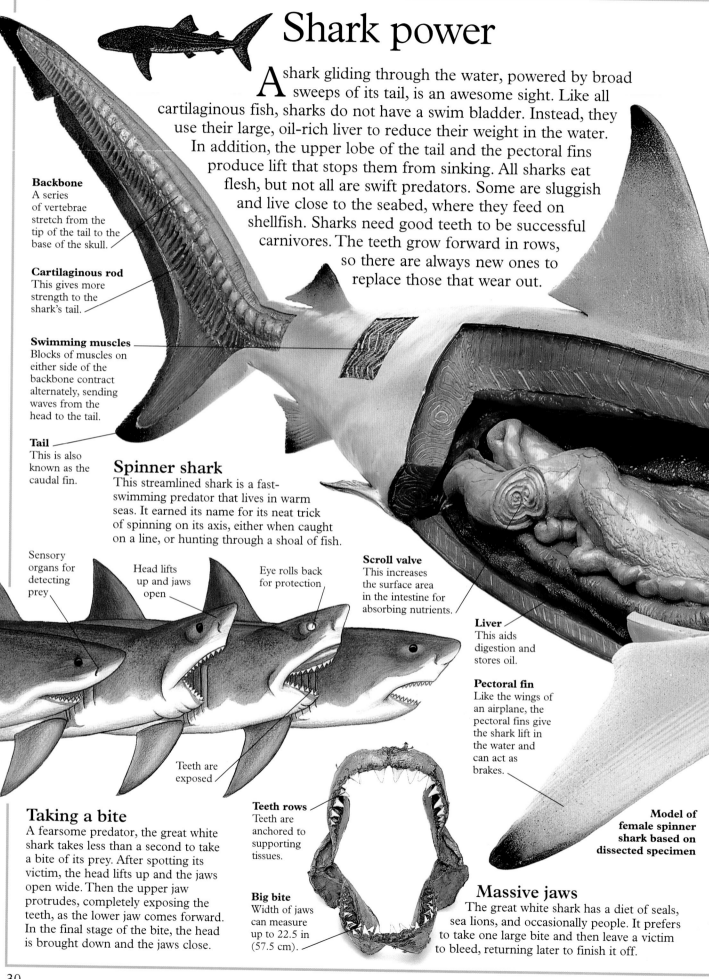

Shark power

A shark gliding through the water, powered by broad sweeps of its tail, is an awesome sight. Like all cartilaginous fish, sharks do not have a swim bladder. Instead, they use their large, oil-rich liver to reduce their weight in the water. In addition, the upper lobe of the tail and the pectoral fins produce lift that stops them from sinking. All sharks eat flesh, but not all are swift predators. Some are sluggish and live close to the seabed, where they feed on shellfish. Sharks need good teeth to be successful carnivores. The teeth grow forward in rows, so there are always new ones to replace those that wear out.

Backbone
A series of vertebrae stretch from the tip of the tail to the base of the skull.

Cartilaginous rod
This gives more strength to the shark's tail.

Swimming muscles
Blocks of muscles on either side of the backbone contract alternately, sending waves from the head to the tail.

Tail
This is also known as the caudal fin.

Spinner shark
This streamlined shark is a fast-swimming predator that lives in warm seas. It earned its name for its neat trick of spinning on its axis, either when caught on a line, or hunting through a shoal of fish.

Sensory organs for detecting prey

Head lifts up and jaws open

Eye rolls back for protection

Scroll valve
This increases the surface area in the intestine for absorbing nutrients.

Liver
This aids digestion and stores oil.

Pectoral fin
Like the wings of an airplane, the pectoral fins give the shark lift in the water and can act as brakes.

Teeth are exposed

Model of female spinner shark based on dissected specimen

Taking a bite
A fearsome predator, the great white shark takes less than a second to take a bite of its prey. After spotting its victim, the head lifts up and the jaws open wide. Then the upper jaw protrudes, completely exposing the teeth, as the lower jaw comes forward. In the final stage of the bite, the head is brought down and the jaws close.

Teeth rows
Teeth are anchored to supporting tissues.

Big bite
Width of jaws can measure up to 22.5 in (57.5 cm).

Massive jaws
The great white shark has a diet of seals, sea lions, and occasionally people. It prefers to take one large bite and then leave a victim to bleed, returning later to finish it off.

Head like a hammer

It is unclear why hammerhead sharks sometimes swim around in groups, or schools, but it may help in their search for a mate. The eyes of the shark are set far apart on each tip of its hammer projections. As it swims along, it swings its head back and forth so that it can see what is happening in all directions.

Whale shark

The largest fish in the sea, a whale shark measures at least 39 ft (12 m) when fully grown. Gentle giants, whale sharks have tiny teeth and feed by straining small fish out of the water.

Cartilage

The skeleton of a shark is made of gristlelike cartilage. This has a different structure than true bone, but can still be hard. In places that need extra strength, like the vertebrae and teeth, it is reinforced with minerals.

Big bones
Vertebrae of the second largest fish, the basking shark, are enormous.

Sandpaper
Smooth in one direction and rough in the other, shark skin used to be used to polish wood.

Denticles

Shark skin does not have flat scales like a bony fish, instead it is covered in tiny teethlike points called denticles. Like shark teeth, the denticles are continuously replaced.

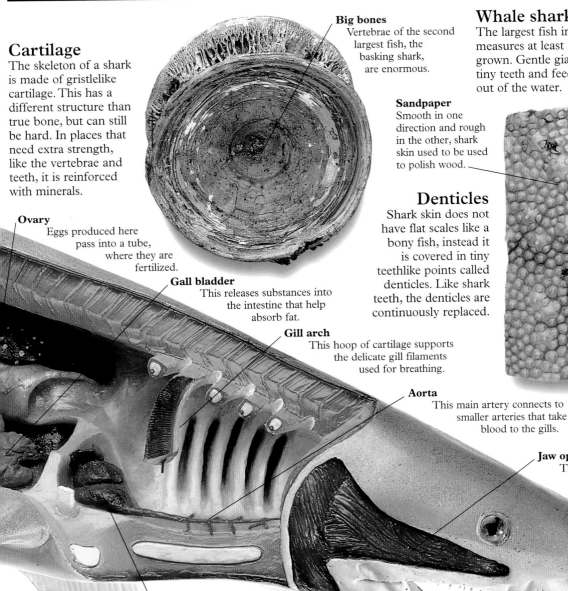

Ovary
Eggs produced here pass into a tube, where they are fertilized.

Gall bladder
This releases substances into the intestine that help absorb fat.

Gill arch
This hoop of cartilage supports the delicate gill filaments used for breathing.

Aorta
This main artery connects to smaller arteries that take blood to the gills.

Jaw opening muscles
These pull the jaw forward in preparation for the shark to take a bite.

Heart
This pumps blood to the gills and all around the body.

Tongue
This is a rigid structure, supported by a pad of cartilage.

Nostril
Water is taken in through the nostrils so that the shark can detect the smells of any nearby prey.

Great white shark tooth

Tiger shark tooth

White shark tooth

School shark tooth

Types of teeth

Shark teeth are often serrated for slicing through flesh. Slender points pierce, while broad, blunt surfaces are used for crushing. Tiger shark teeth have both a pointed and a cutting edge to deal well with a variety of food.

Filtering and feeding

Rising to the surface in a great sea of bubbles, humpback whales feed on a swarming mass of shrimplike creatures called krill. Humpbacks are baleen whales, which filter their food through a series of fringed plates in the mouth. In places where there is a plentiful supply of food, the humpbacks simply swim along open-mouthed, lunging through the surface of the sea to let the water drain out of their mouths. However, at other times, humpbacks are unique in using a bubble-net fishing technique that herds the krill into a concentrated mass for them to gulp down. In the summer months baleen whales stock up on food in the cold polar waters. They migrate to warmer waters in winter to breed.

Big gulp
Over 528 gallons (2,000 liters) of water and food – enough to fill a small room – are taken into the mouth as the throat expands.

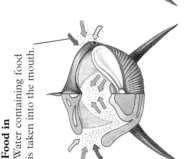

Food in
Water containing food is taken into the mouth.

Water out
When the mouth shuts, the large tongue is raised and forces the water out through the baleen plates.

Filter feeding
In food-rich areas, a baleen whale swims along with its mouth slightly open, taking in big gulps of seawater. When the mouth is shut, water filters out through the baleen plates, leaving food trapped there. From time to time, the enormous, fleshy tongue wipes off the food, and the whale swallows it down.

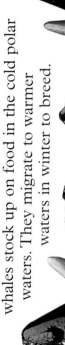

Bubble net
Humpback whales start to circle beneath a shoal of krill. As they swim, they release a stream of bubbles, creating a "net" in which the krill are herded. The whales rise up through the center of the net with their mouths wide open, gulping water that is full of food.

Flippers
The humpback whale has exceptionally long flippers.

Ball of krill
The swirling bubbles frighten the krill and drive them into the center of the net.

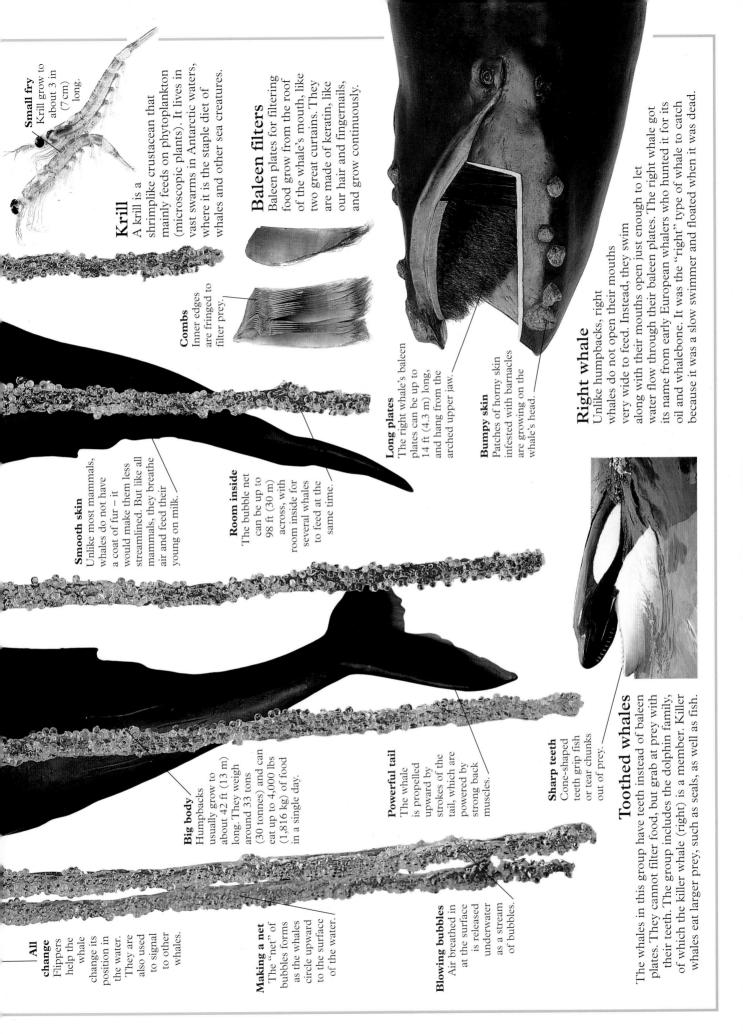

Small fry
Krill grow to about 3 in (7cm) long.

Krill

A krill is a shrimplike crustacean that mainly feeds on phytoplankton (microscopic plants). It lives in vast swarms in Antarctic waters, where it is the staple diet of whales and other sea creatures.

Baleen filters

Baleen plates for filtering food grow from the roof of the whale's mouth, like two great curtains. They are made of keratin, like our hair and fingernails, and grow continuously.

Combs
Inner edges are fringed to filter prey.

Long plates
The right whale's baleen plates can be up to 14 ft (4.3 m) long, and hang from the arched upper jaw.

Bumpy skin
Patches of horny skin infested with barnacles are growing on the whale's head.

Right whale

Unlike humpbacks, right whales do not open their mouths very wide to feed. Instead, they swim along with their mouths open just enough to let water flow through their baleen plates. The right whale got its name from early European whalers who hunted it for its oil and whalebone. It was the "right" type of whale to catch because it was a slow swimmer and floated when it was dead.

Smooth skin
Unlike most mammals, whales do not have a coat of fur – it would make them less streamlined. But like all mammals, they breathe air and feed their young on milk.

Room inside
The bubble net can be up to 98 ft (30 m) across, with room inside for several whales to feed at the same time.

All change
Flippers help the whale change its position in the water. They are also used to signal to other whales.

Making a net
The "net" of bubbles forms as the whales circle upward to the surface of the water.

Big body
Humpbacks usually grow to about 42 ft (13 m) long. They weigh around 33 tons (30 tonnes) and can eat up to 4,000 lbs (1,816 kg) of food in a single day.

Powerful tail
The whale is propelled upward by strokes of the tail, which are powered by strong back muscles.

Blowing bubbles
Air breathed in at the surface is released underwater as a stream of bubbles.

Sharp teeth
Cone-shaped teeth grip fish or tear chunks out of prey.

Toothed whales

The whales in this group have teeth instead of baleen plates. They cannot filter food, but grab at prey with their teeth. The group includes the dolphin family, of which the killer whale (right) is a member. Killer whales eat larger prey, such as seals, as well as fish.

Riding along

Get close enough to a gray whale as it surfaces to breathe, and patches of barnacles on its head are easy to see. Look closer still, and around the barnacles is a seething mass of whale lice. The lice are crustaceans related to shrimps and crabs. Both the lice and the barnacles irritate the whales, which scrape against rocks to try to dislodge them. The barnacles feed on particles in the water, but the lice do more damage since they feed on the whale's delicate skin tissues. The barnacles produce larvae that drift in the sea until they find another whale to settle on. The lice breed on the whale and the young, like the adults, cling on with hooked claws.

Helping each other
It benefits hermit crabs and anemones to live together. The anemone's stinging tentacles deter attackers, while the hermit crab's leftovers provide anemones with food.

Migrating south
Gray whales spend the summer feeding in the food-rich waters of the North Pacific. In winter, they migrate south along the North American coast to give birth to their calves in warm waters.

Feathery feelers
The handlike feeding limbs catch particles in the water. When enough food is collected, they draw back into the shell and pass it to the mouth.

Brittle plates
A wall of plates protects the barnacle. These are much more brittle than those on shore barnacles.

Whale louse
Creeping over the barnacles, the louse searches for a good spot to feed.

Hooked claws to hang on with

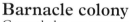

Barnacle colony
Gray whales are encrusted with a type of barnacle that is found only on them. Colonies of these barnacles live on the whale's head, back, and tail, leaving scars on the skin. Hoards of whale lice shelter among the barnacles because the ridged plates provide a good surface for them to cling to.

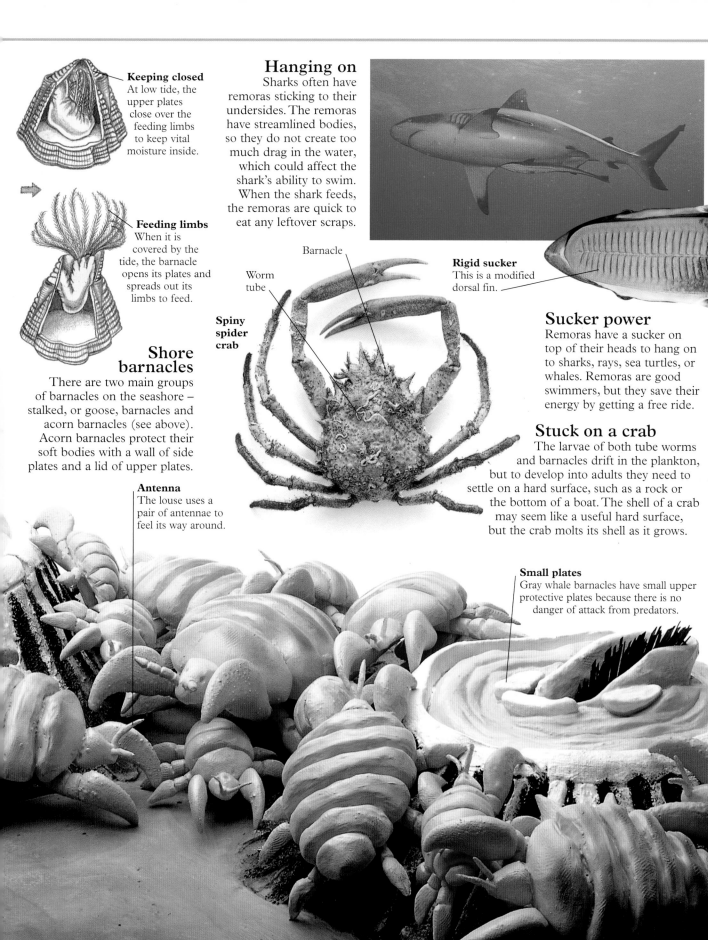

Keeping closed
At low tide, the upper plates close over the feeding limbs to keep vital moisture inside.

Feeding limbs
When it is covered by the tide, the barnacle opens its plates and spreads out its limbs to feed.

Shore barnacles

There are two main groups of barnacles on the seashore – stalked, or goose, barnacles and acorn barnacles (see above). Acorn barnacles protect their soft bodies with a wall of side plates and a lid of upper plates.

Antenna
The louse uses a pair of antennae to feel its way around.

Hanging on

Sharks often have remoras sticking to their undersides. The remoras have streamlined bodies, so they do not create too much drag in the water, which could affect the shark's ability to swim. When the shark feeds, the remoras are quick to eat any leftover scraps.

Barnacle

Worm tube

Spiny spider crab

Rigid sucker
This is a modified dorsal fin.

Sucker power

Remoras have a sucker on top of their heads to hang on to sharks, rays, sea turtles, or whales. Remoras are good swimmers, but they save their energy by getting a free ride.

Stuck on a crab

The larvae of both tube worms and barnacles drift in the plankton, but to develop into adults they need to settle on a hard surface, such as a rock or the bottom of a boat. The shell of a crab may seem like a useful hard surface, but the crab molts its shell as it grows.

Small plates
Gray whale barnacles have small upper protective plates because there is no danger of attack from predators.

Clicks and whistles

Dolphins and other toothed whales use a kind of sonar system to find out what lies ahead of them. Scientists are still learning how the system works. It is likely that click sounds are produced in the dolphin's nasal passages. The sounds bounce off an object and the returning echoes are picked up through the lower jaw. The dolphin can determine where the object is, its size, and its shape by listening to the pattern of the echoes. Dolphins use whistles to keep in contact with members of their social group. Baleen whales also make noises, but they do not have the sophisticated sonar system of toothed whales.

Baby noises
Every bottlenose dolphin has a unique whistle that it learns as a youngster. The "signature whistle" of a male calf sounds similar to that of its mother. Dolphins whistle to locate one another.

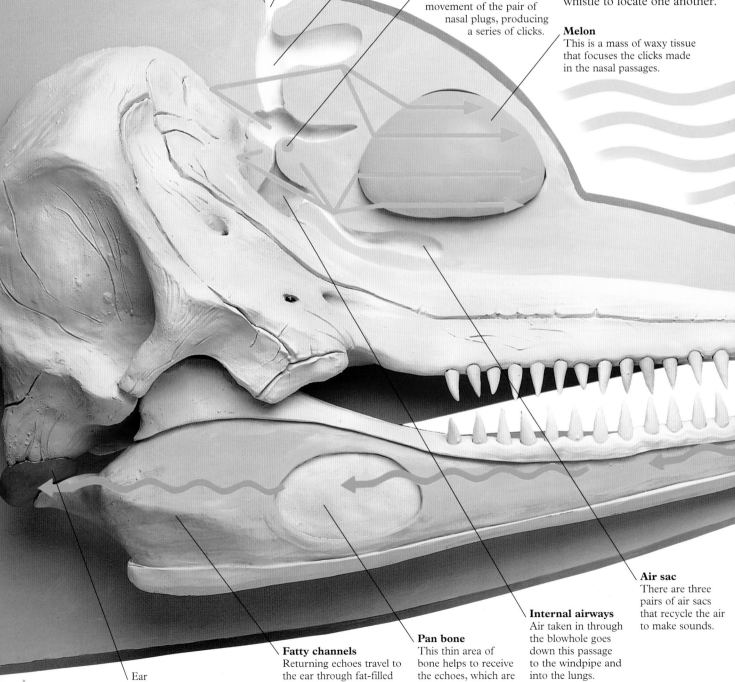

Blowhole

Nasal passage

Nasal plug
Air pressure causes movement of the pair of nasal plugs, producing a series of clicks.

Melon
This is a mass of waxy tissue that focuses the clicks made in the nasal passages.

Air sac
There are three pairs of air sacs that recycle the air to make sounds.

Internal airways
Air taken in through the blowhole goes down this passage to the windpipe and into the lungs.

Pan bone
This thin area of bone helps to receive the echoes, which are then sent to the ear.

Fatty channels
Returning echoes travel to the ear through fat-filled channels in the lower jaw.

Ear

The whale's song
Male humpback whales sing to attract a mate and to defend their territory against other males. The songs differ between oceans, but the individual whales in a population sing the same song, which changes during the season.

Outgoing sounds
A dolphin can make many click sounds a second, increasing the rate as it approaches an object.

Killer whale dialects
Members of a group, or pod, of killer whales stay together for a lifetime. Each pod has a set of calls. Their unique calls, or dialects, probably help them keep in touch with other members of their group.

Fish prey
An object swimming in front of the dolphin blocks some of the outgoing sound.

Returning waves
Some of the sound bounces back from the fish prey toward the dolphin.

Elephant rumble
Varying between 10–20 Hz, these sounds can travel about 2 km (3 mi).

Echolocation
Clicks made in the nasal passage are focused by the melon into a beam of sound. When the sound beam hits an object, some of the sound bounces back toward the dolphin. These echoes are picked up by the lower jaw bone and transmitted through fatty channels to the ear.

Dolphin clicks
These are made up to 200,000 Hz and sometimes at even higher frequencies.

Baby scream
This is made at about 3,000 Hz.

Time

Amplitude

Social life
Atlantic spotted dolphins live in clear water where people can observe their social lives. These dolphins are generally found in groups, or schools, of up to 60 animals. Identifying which dolphin makes a sound is hard because they do not open their mouths to make a noise.

High and low sounds
Humans can hear sounds from 20–20,000 Hz (cycles per second), which means they cannot hear very low-pitched or high-pitched noises. Toothed whales, including dolphins, use high-pitched sounds in their sonar systems.

Poison darts

The poison used by animals in their stings or spines is called venom. Many animals use venom to subdue their prey or to defend themselves. Cone snails hunt at night around coral reefs, waiting to jab dartlike teeth loaded with venom into their prey. Within seconds, the venom paralyzes the victim, which is then engulfed by the snail's greatly expanded food tube. The teeth are used one at a time and several may be needed to subdue the fish prey, so the cone snail has a never-ending store at the ready. The teeth are also used for defense, so it is unwise to pick up the shell of a cone snail in case its owner is still living inside.

Sea slug
The glaucus sea slug actually eats the Portuguese man-of-war, a relative of jellyfish that is well known for its stings. The sea slug recycles the nasty stings and uses them for its own protection.

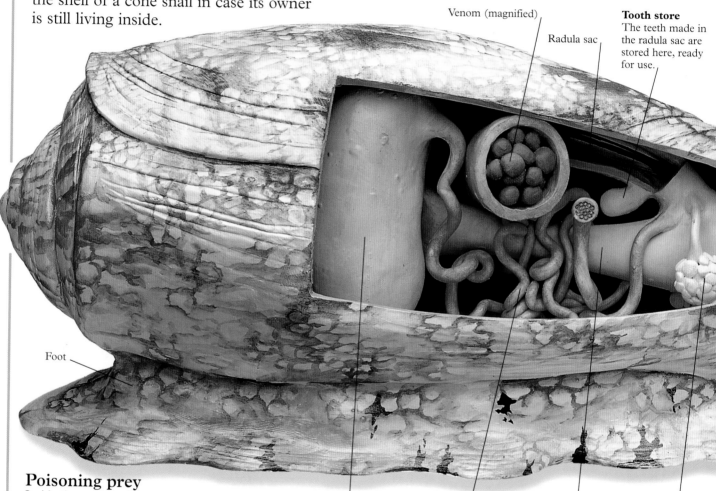

Venom (magnified)

Radula sac

Tooth store
The teeth made in the radula sac are stored here, ready for use.

Foot

Poisoning prey
Inside the cone snail are a number of organs that it uses to poison its prey. A tooth travels from the tooth store via the throat to the tip of the snout. The hollow tooth is flushed with venom as it jabs into prey.

Venom bulb
Muscles in the walls of this fluid-filled bulb contract to flush venom out of the venom gland.

Venom gland
Granules of venom are made in this ductlike gland.

Throat
The base of the snout opens into a swollen throat.

Salivary gland
The substances used to digest the cone snail's prey are produced in the salivary gland.

Deadly cones
Cone snails that feed on fish have stronger venom than those that eat worms or other snails. A few fish-eating cone snails, like the geography cone (left), can even kill people with their venom.

Venomous urchin
Sea urchins are covered in prickly spines for defense, but certain kinds are also equipped with venom for extra protection. This urchin has venom glands on its spines as well as on the tiny pincers, which are called pedicellariae.

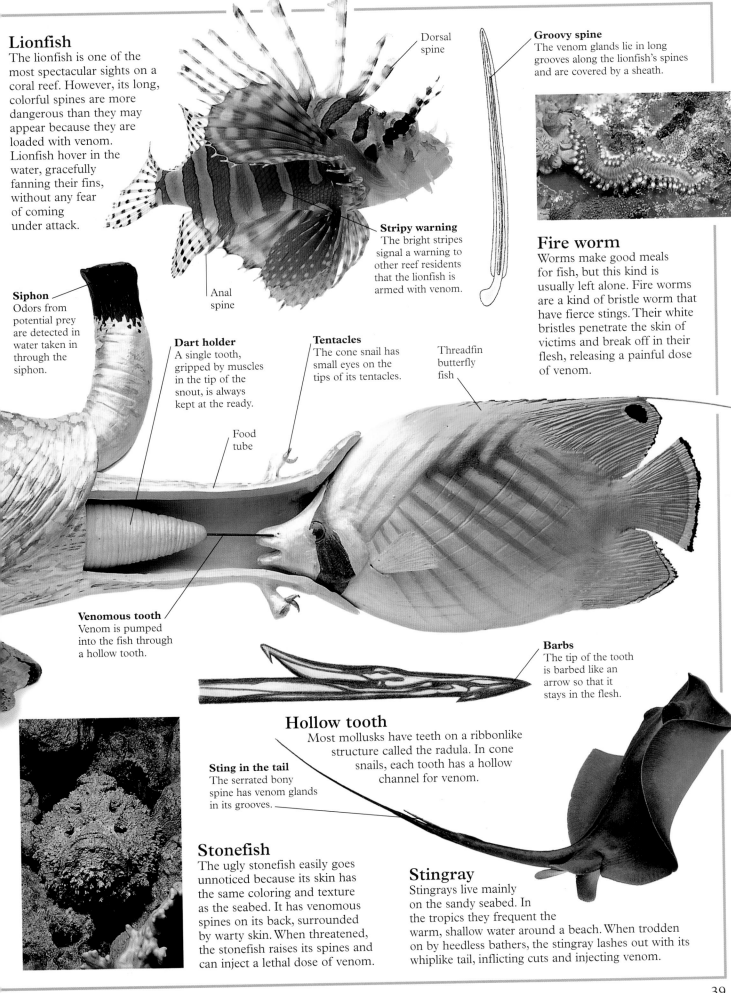

Lionfish

The lionfish is one of the most spectacular sights on a coral reef. However, its long, colorful spines are more dangerous than they may appear because they are loaded with venom. Lionfish hover in the water, gracefully fanning their fins, without any fear of coming under attack.

Dorsal spine

Groovy spine
The venom glands lie in long grooves along the lionfish's spines and are covered by a sheath.

Stripy warning
The bright stripes signal a warning to other reef residents that the lionfish is armed with venom.

Anal spine

Fire worm

Worms make good meals for fish, but this kind is usually left alone. Fire worms are a kind of bristle worm that have fierce stings. Their white bristles penetrate the skin of victims and break off in their flesh, releasing a painful dose of venom.

Siphon
Odors from potential prey are detected in water taken in through the siphon.

Dart holder
A single tooth, gripped by muscles in the tip of the snout, is always kept at the ready.

Tentacles
The cone snail has small eyes on the tips of its tentacles.

Food tube

Threadfin butterfly fish

Venomous tooth
Venom is pumped into the fish through a hollow tooth.

Barbs
The tip of the tooth is barbed like an arrow so that it stays in the flesh.

Hollow tooth

Most mollusks have teeth on a ribbonlike structure called the radula. In cone snails, each tooth has a hollow channel for venom.

Sting in the tail
The serrated bony spine has venom glands in its grooves.

Stonefish

The ugly stonefish easily goes unnoticed because its skin has the same coloring and texture as the seabed. It has venomous spines on its back, surrounded by warty skin. When threatened, the stonefish raises its spines and can inject a lethal dose of venom.

Stingray

Stingrays live mainly on the sandy seabed. In the tropics they frequent the warm, shallow water around a beach. When trodden on by heedless bathers, the stingray lashes out with its whiplike tail, inflicting cuts and injecting venom.

Water babies

Most sea creatures mate to produce their young, but some, like sea anemones, reproduce without mating. Some parents give their offspring a head start by caring for the developing youngsters. Some of the most devoted parents are sea horses. Males become pregnant – instead of shedding thousands of eggs into the water like many fish, female sea horses pass their eggs to a male, who fertilizes them and keeps them safe in his brood pouch. Sea horses remain faithful to one partner during at least a season, only seeking another in case of death. Sadly, sea horses are at risk because there is a prosperous trade in their dried bodies.

Dorsal fin
The sea horse swims along in an upright position by beating this fin.

Blending in
The color of the sea horse's skin can change to match its surroundings.

1 A pair of sea horses can court for up to nine hours before actually mating. Flashing bright colors, they entwine tails or twirl around a stem. In the final stages of courtship, they swim upward, facing each other. The female places her eggs in the male's brood pouch through a tubelike organ called an ovipositor.

2 Inside the pouch, the eggs are fertilized by the male's sperm. The eggs become embedded in the pouch's spongy lining. The pouch provides the embryos with oxygen and nourishment.

Splitting up
Anemones can reproduce by simply dividing in two. They also produce eggs that are fertilized by sperm. Fertilization can occur either in the water or in the body cavity, in which case the young are born through the parent's mouth.

Skin tendrils
These help camouflage the sea horse.

Young prawn
This prawn larva does not look much like its parents. After going through several stages of development, the youngster stops drifting in the plankton and settles on the seabed to become an adult.

In the pouch
Most types of sea horses carry between 100 to 200 eggs at one time.

Guarding the eggs
Sergeant major damsel fish glue their eggs to a rock. The male guards the eggs until they have hatched and removes any that are not developing properly. He also keeps away other fish that may try to eat the eggs.

Staying together
The mother whale keeps close to her calf.

Big baby
When a baby blue whale is born, it measures about 23 ft (7 m) long and can weigh up to 3 tons, making it the largest baby in the ocean. It takes about 12 months from the time when the egg is fertilized inside the mother to the birth of the baby whale.

Contractions
The pouch wall contracts, forcing the young out through its opening.

Newly born
Youngsters are usually born at night. Even then they are vulnerable and many will not survive.

3 Like many fish embryos, the developing sea horse has an egg sac that provides it with some nourishment. The female will visit her mate throughout his pregnancy.

4 Around the halfway stage of its development, the embryo still has a large egg sac. The fins start to develop and the eyes become prominent. The tail fills out with muscles.

Embryo
The developing embryo sticks to a membrane as well as to the lining of the brood pouch.

5 The egg sac is nearly used up. The sea horse's characteristic snout begins to develop. Once born, it will use the snout to suck up creatures from the seawater.

6 After two to six weeks (according to the temperature and type of sea horse), the young are born. The male labors for hours, giving birth to the young in spurts. When they have all been released, the sea horse flushes out his pouch, preparing it for the next batch of eggs.

Pouch wall
As the embryos grow, the pouch wall expands.

Tail clings to support

Glossary

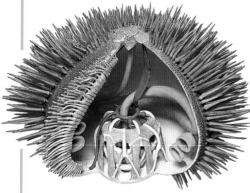

Sea urchin

A

Algae
A group of plants that have no roots, stems, or leaves, ranging in size from microscopic plants such as diatoms, to large seaweeds such as kelps.

B

Baleen whales
A group of toothless whales that strain their food through fringed plates.

Buoyancy
The ability to float in liquid. To achieve this, fish use a swim bladder. Sharks use an oil-rich liver.

C

Cartilaginous fish
Fish such as sharks and rays that have skeletons made of a gristlelike substance called cartilage.

Cephalopods
A group of mollusks that have a head surrounded by a ring of tentacles. Includes octopuses, squid, nautiluses, and cuttlefish.

Cnidarians
A group of animals that have stinging cells called nematocysts. Includes corals, sea anemones, and jellyfish.

Continental shelf
The shallow seabed around the continental margin, not usually more that 656 ft (200 m) deep.

Crustaceans
A group of animals that have a hard outer skeleton, jointed limbs, and two pairs of feelers in front of their mouths. Includes lobsters, shrimps, and crabs.

Current
The natural movement of seawater, not caused by tides.

E

Echinoderms
A group of animals that have a five-rayed body plan, tube feet, and lack a head. Includes starfish and sea urchins.

Echolocation
A sonar system used by animals such as dolphins to determine the position of an object by making sounds and picking up the pattern of echoes reflected back.

Embryo
An early stage in the development of an animal that occurs before birth.

Enzyme
A substance that sets off a chemical reaction without being used up itself in the process.

Chambered nautilus

F

Food chain
A chain of organisms through which energy is transferred. Plants are at the beginning of the chain, followed by plant-eating animals, which are in turn eaten by larger animals, and so on.

Deep-sea floor

Funnel
A flexible tubelike structure present in cephalopods through which water is expelled. Its position in the water controls the direction of swimming.

G

Gills
Delicate structures through which animals breathe underwater. Gills absorb oxygen from the water and release waste carbon dioxide back into the water.

H

Herbivore
A plant-eating animal.

I

Invertebrates
Animals without backbones, such as cnidarians, crustaceans, echinoderms, mollusks, and worms.

J

Jet propulsion
The means by which an animal moves in water by releasing a jet of water.

L

Larva
A young stage in the development of many invertebrates, which can look quite different from the adult.

M

Mammals
A group of animals that are covered in fur or hair and feed their young on milk.

Mantle
A layer of tissue that covers the soft body parts of a mollusk. It secretes the shell in species where one is present and controls the flow of water in and out of the animal.

Migration
The movement of an animal or group of animals from one location to another. It often takes place in certain seasons.

Mollusks
A group of animals that have soft bodies surrounded by a layer of tissue called the mantle. Includes clams, snails, chitons, squid, and nautiluses.

Sea horse brood pouch

Mucus
A slimy substance that is produced by animals to help them capture prey.

N

Nematocyst
A microscopic stinging cell present in cnidarians that is used for defense or to capture food.

Nutrients
Substances that give nourishment to all living things.

O

Ovipositor
A tubelike structure through which eggs are laid or transferred.

P

Parasite
An animal that lives in close association with another, getting food from it and sometimes causing it harm.

Pedicellaria
A pincerlike structure found on the skin of some kinds of echinoderms, such as sea urchins.

Plankton
Microscopic plants and animals that drift in the water, providing a supply of food for many other animals.

Pod
A group, or school, of seals or whales.

Polyp
The anemonelike form of cnidarians, such as a sea anemone or a single coral animal, consisting of a cylindrical hollow body with tentacles around the mouth.

Predator
A carnivorous (meat-eating) animal that preys on and eats other animals.

S

Sediment
Small particles of rock and other kinds of matter that are gradually deposited at the bottom of the sea.

Sponge
An animal with a porous structure and a skeleton made of interlocking fibers.

T

Tentacle
A long, flexible structure found around the mouth of anemones, squid, and other invertebrates that is used for feeding and grasping things.

Humpback whales bubble-net fishing

V

Venom
Poison made by animals, often transferred by a bite or sting.

Vertebrates
Animals with backbones and skulls, such as fish, amphibians, birds, reptiles, and mammals.

Volcano
An opening through the Earth's surface through which molten material and gases may erupt.

Z

Zones
The different depths of the ocean that have characteristic plants and animals, suited to the availability of light and the temperature of the water.

Zooplankton
The animal part of plankton.

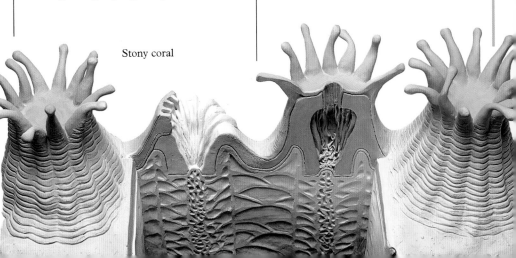

Stony coral

Index

Acknowledgments

Thanks to:
Brian Bett for checking the models. The following specialists: Vincent Janik on dolphins; Brian Rosen on corals; John Taylor on cone shells; Amanda Vincent on sea horses. Geoffrey Waller for dissecting the shark and for guidance and advice. Marion Dent for the index.

Design assistance:
Goldberry Broad and Alex Clifford

Photographic assistance:
Dave Morgan

Illustrations:
John Woodcock 9;17;18; 29; 37; 39;tl; Dominic Zwemmer 11; 23; 30; 32; 35; 39bc; 42; Angelica Elsebach 25

Picture Credits:
Key: t=top; b=below; c=center; l=left; r=right; a=above
Bruce Coleman: Erik Bjurstrom 16cr; Jane Burton 14c, 34tr; Jett Foott 19c; Jens Rydell 23tl; Nancy Sefton 16cl **FLPA:** K. Aitken/Panda VC 148881D 16t; Mark Conlin 9tr; Peter David 21bl; Mark Nekman 14t; Marineland 36tr; R.

Pitman/Earthvions 37tr; D.P. Wilson 9tc **Images Colour Library:** Endpapers, 8tr; 26b **Natural History Museum, London:** 41c **Naturpress, Madrid:** © Jorge J. Candán 21cr, 26cl, 28bl; © Alberto Ramos 35tr **Oxford Scientific Films:** © Tony Bomford 31tr; John Cheverton 40bl; Zig Leszczynski **Planet Earth:** Pete Atkinson 10bl,19t; Robert Arnold 41tl; Georgette Douwma 38br; Pieter Folkens ©1944 34cl; Robert Hessler 9b; A. Kerstitch 24cl; Ken Lucas 20bl, 33c; 35cra; David Maitland 38tr; Mary Snyderman 31tl, 41tr; Peter

Scoones 14b, 39bl; © Denise Tackett 24b; © Larry Tackett 25cr; Hewarth Voigtmann 23tr; James D. Watt 28bl; Bill Wood 19ac; Norbert Wu 39tr, 40cl **The Telegraph Colour Library:** Planet Earth/James D. Watt 37tl **Tony Stone:** Mike Severns 10cl **Townsville Hospital, Australia:** 15t

Every effort has been made to trace the copyright holders. DK apologizes for any unintentional omissions and would be pleased, in such cases, to add an acknowledgment in future editions.